✠

BENEDICT XVI

Way of the Cross

✠

Pauline
BOOKS & MEDIA
Boston

Library of Congress Cataloging-in-Publication Data

Benedict XVI, Pope, 1927–
Way of the Cross / by Benedict XVI.
      p. cm.
ISBN 0-8198-8308-5 (pbk. : alk. paper)
1. Stations of the Cross. 2. Jesus Christ—Passion. 3. Catholic Church—Prayer-books and devotions—English. I. Title.
BX2040.B43 2005
232.96—dc22

                2005014951

Vatican Translation

Cover design by Helen Rita Lane, FSP

Photo of Benedict XVI courtesy of Sergia Ballini, FSP

Artwork courtesy of Saint Bernulpus Parish, Oosterbeek, the Netherlands.

Special thanks to M. W. J. Willems and Luc van den Hemel.

Published by Pauline Books & Media, 50 Saint Paul's Avenue, Boston, MA 02130-3491. www.pauline.org

Printed in Korea

Pauline Books & Media is the publishing house of the Daughters of St. Paul, an international congregation of women religious serving the Church with the communications media.

1 2 3 4 5 6 7 8 9   11 10 09 08 07 06 05

Office for the Liturgical Celebrations
of the Supreme Pontiff

WAY OF THE CROSS
AT THE COLOSSEUM

GOOD FRIDAY 2005

Meditations and Prayers by
Benedict XVI

PRESENTATION

$\mathcal{T}$he *leitmotiv* of the present Way of the Cross appears immediately in the opening prayer, and again at the Fourteenth Station. It is found in the words spoken by Jesus on Palm Sunday, after entering Jerusalem, in reply to the question of some Greeks who sought to see him: "Unless a grain of wheat falls to the earth and dies, it remains alone; but if it dies, it bears much fruit" (Jn 12:24). In this saying, the Lord compares the course of his whole earthly existence to that of a grain of wheat, which only by dying can produce fruit. He interprets his earthly life, his death, and his resurrection from the standpoint of the Most Holy Eucharist, which recapitulates his entire mystery. He had experienced his death as an act of self-oblation, an act of love, and his body was then transfigured in the new life of the resurrection. He, the Incarnate Word, now becomes our food, food that leads to true life, life eternal. The Eternal Word—the power that creates life—comes down from heaven as the true manna, the bread bestowed upon man in faith and in sacrament. The Way of the Cross is thus a path leading to the heart of the Eucharistic mystery: popular piety and sacramental piety of the Church blend together and become one. The prayer of the Way of the Cross is a path leading to a deep spiritual communion with Jesus; lacking this, our sacramental communion would remain empty. The Way of the Cross is thus a "mystagogical" way.

This vision contrasts with a purely sentimental approach to the Way of the Cross. In the Eighth Station our Lord speaks of this danger to the women of Jerusalem who weep for him. Mere sentiment is never enough; the Way of the Cross ought to be a school of faith, the faith that by its very nature "works through love" (Gal 5:6). This is not to say that sentiment does not have its proper place. The Fathers considered heartlessness to be the primary vice of the pagans, and they appealed to the vision of Ezekiel, who announced to the people of Israel God's promise to take away their hearts of stone and to give them hearts of flesh (cf. Ez 11:19).

In the Way of the Cross we see a God who shares in human sufferings, a God whose love does not remain aloof and distant, but comes into our midst, even enduring death on a cross (cf. Phil 2:8). The God who shares our sufferings, the God who became man in order to bear our cross, wants to transform our hearts of stone; he invites us to share in the sufferings of others. He wants to give us a "heart of flesh" that will not remain stony before the suffering of others, but can be touched and led to the love that heals and restores.

Here, once again, we return to the words of Jesus about the grain of wheat, which he himself laid down as the fundamental axiom of the Christian life: "He who loves his life loses it, and he who hates his life in this world will keep it for eternal life" (Jn 12:25; cf. Mt 16:25; Mk 8:35; Lk 9:24 and 17:33: "Whoever seeks to gain his life will lose it, but whoever loses his life will preserve it"). We also see more clearly the meaning of the words that, in the Synoptic Gospels, precede this summation of Christ's message: "If any man would come after me, let him deny himself and take up his cross and follow me" (Mt 16:24). Jesus himself interpreted for us the meaning of the "Way of the Cross"; he taught us how to pray it and follow it: the Way of the Cross is the path of losing ourselves, the path of true love. On this path he has gone before us; on it he teaches us how to pray the Way of the Cross. Once again we come back to the grain of wheat, to the Most Holy Eucharist, in which the fruits of Christ's death and Resurrection are continually made present in our midst. In the Eucharist Jesus walks at our side, as he did with the disciples of Emmaus, making himself ever anew a part of our history.

Opening Prayer

*L*ord Jesus Christ, for our sake you became like the grain of wheat that falls to the earth and dies, so that it may bear much fruit (cf. Jn 12:24). You invited us to follow you along this path when you told us "the one who loves his life loses it, and the one who hates his life in this world will keep it for eternal life" (Jn 12:25). Yet we are attached to our life. We do not want to abandon it; we want to keep it all for ourselves. We want to hold on to it, not to give it away. But you go before us, showing us that it is only by giving away our life that we can save it.

As we walk with you on the Way of the Cross, you lead us along the way of the grain of wheat, the way of a fruitfulness that leads to eternity. The cross—our self-offering—weighs heavily upon us. Along your own Way of the Cross you also carried my cross. Nor did you carry it just at one distant moment in the past, for your love continues to accompany every moment of my life. Today you carry that cross with me and for me, and, amazingly, you want me, like Simon of Cyrene, to join you in carrying your cross; you want me to walk at your side and place myself with you at the service of the world's redemption.

Grant that my Way of the Cross may not be just a moment of passing piety. Help all of us to accompany you not only with noble thoughts, but with all our hearts and in every step we take each day of our lives. Help us resolutely to set out on the Way of the Cross and to persevere on your path. Free us from the fear of the cross, from the fear of mockery, from the fear that our life may escape our grasp unless we cling possessively to everything it has to offer. Help us to unmask all those temptations that promise life, but whose enticements in the end leave us only empty and deluded. Help us not to take life, but to give it. As you accompany us on the path of the grain of wheat, help us to discover, in "losing our lives," the path of love, the path that gives us true life, and life in abundance (Jn 10:10).

✠

FIRST STATION

Jesus is condemned to death

℣. *Adoramus te, Christe, et benedicimus tibi.*
℞. *Quia per sanctam crucem tuam redemisti mundum.*

℣. *We adore you, O Christ, and we bless you.*
℞. *Because by your holy cross you have redeemed the world.*

From the Gospel according to Matthew 27:22–23, 26

Pilate said to them, "Then what should I do with Jesus who is called the Messiah?" All of them said, "Let him be crucified!" Then he asked, "Why, what evil has he done?" But they shouted all the more, "Let him be crucified!" So he released Barabbas for them; and after flogging Jesus, he handed him over to be crucified.

MEDITATION

The Judge of the world, who will come again to judge us all, stands there, dishonored and defenseless before an earthly judge. Pilate is not utterly evil. He knows that the condemned man is innocent, and he looks for a way to free him.

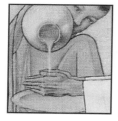 But his heart is divided. And in the end he lets his own position, his own self-interest, prevail over what is right. Nor are the men who are shouting and demanding the death of Jesus utterly evil. Many of them, on the day of Pentecost, will feel "cut to the heart" (Acts 2:37), when Peter will say to them: "Jesus of Nazareth, a man attested to you by God...you crucified and killed by the hands of those outside the law" (Acts 2:22ff.). But at that moment they are caught up in the crowd. They are shouting because everyone else is shouting, and they are shouting the same thing that everyone else is shouting. And in this way, justice is trampled underfoot by weakness, cowardice, and fear of the dictate of the ruling mindset. The quiet

voice of conscience is drowned out by the cries of the crowd. Evil draws its power from indecision and concern for what other people think.

PRAYER

Lord, you were condemned to death because fear of what other people may think suppressed the voice of conscience. So too, throughout history, the innocent have always been maltreat-ed, condemned, and killed. How many times have we ourselves preferred success to the truth, our reputation to justice? Strengthen the quiet voice of our conscience, your own voice, in  our lives. Look at us as you looked at Peter after his denial. Let your gaze penetrate our hearts and indicate the direction our lives must take. On the day of Pentecost you stirred the hearts of those who, on Good Friday, clamored for your death, and you brought them to conversion. In this way you gave hope to all. Grant us, ever anew, the grace of conversion.

All:

Our Father, who art in heaven,
hallowed be thy name;
thy kingdom come;
thy will be done on earth as it is in heaven.
Give us this day our daily bread;
and forgive us our trespasses
as we forgive those who trespass against us;
and lead us not into temptation,
but deliver us from evil.

Stabat Mater

Stabat Mater dolorosa,
iuxta crucem lacrimosa,
dum pendebat Filius.

At the cross her station keeping,
stood the mournful Mother weeping,
close to Jesus to the last.

✝

SECOND STATION

*Jesus takes up
his cross*

℣. *Adoramus te, Christe, et benedicimus tibi.*
℞. *Quia per sanctam crucem tuam redemisti mundum.*

℣. *We adore you, O Christ, and we bless you.*
℞. *Because by your holy cross you have redeemed the world.*

From the Gospel according to Matthew 27:27–31

Then the soldiers of the governor took Jesus into the governor's headquarters, and they gathered the whole cohort around him. They stripped him and put a scarlet robe on him, and after twisting some thorns into a crown, they put it on his head. They put a reed in his right hand and knelt before him and mocked him, saying, "Hail, King of the Jews!" They spat on him, and took the reed and struck him on the head. After mocking him, they stripped him of

the robe and put his own clothes on him.
Then they led him away to crucify him.

MEDITATION

Jesus, condemned as an imposter king, is mocked, but this very mockery lays bare a painful truth. How often are the symbols of power, borne by the great ones of this world, an  affront to truth, to justice, and to the dignity of humanity! How many times are their pomp and their lofty words nothing but grandiose lies, a parody of their solemn obliga-tion to serve the common good! It is because Jesus is mocked and wears the crown of suf-fering that he appears as the true King. His scepter is justice (cf. Ps 45:7). The price of justice in this world is suffering: Jesus, the true King, does not reign through violence, but through a love that suffers for us and with us. He takes up the cross, our cross, the burden of being human, the burden of the world. And so he goes before us and points out to us the way that leads to true life.

PRAYER

*L*ord, you willingly subjected yourself to mockery and scorn. Help us not to ally ourselves with those who look down on the weak and suffering. Help us to acknowledge your face in the lowly and the outcast. May we never lose heart when faced with the contempt of this  world, which ridicules our obedience to your will. You carried your own cross, and you ask us to follow you on this path (cf. Mt 10:38). Help us to take up the cross and not to shun it. May we never complain or become discouraged by life's trials. Help us to follow the path of love and, in submitting to its demands, to find true joy.

All:

Our Father, who art in heaven,
hallowed be thy name;
thy kingdom come;
thy will be done on earth as it is in heaven.
Give us this day our daily bread;
and forgive us our trespasses
as we forgive those who trespass against us;
and lead us not into temptation,
but deliver us from evil.

Stabat Mater

Cuius animam gementem,
contristatam et dolentem
pertransivit gladius.

Through her heart, his sorrow sharing,
all his bitter anguish bearing,
now at length the sword had passed.

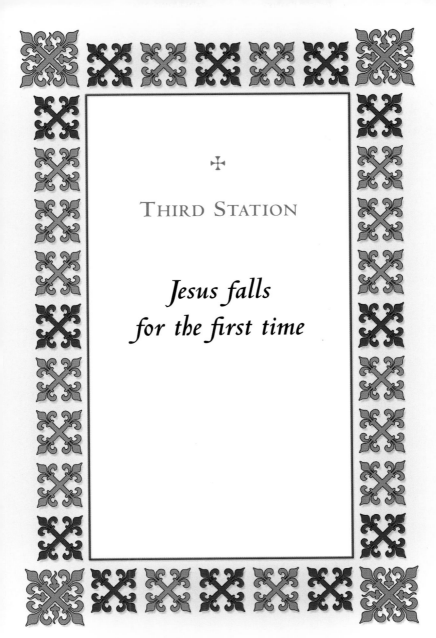

☩

THIRD STATION

Jesus falls for the first time

℣. Adoramus te, Christe, et benedicimus tibi.
℞. Quia per sanctam crucem tuam redemisti mundum.

℣. We adore you, O Christ, and we bless you.
℞. Because by your holy cross you have redeemed the world.

From the Book of the Prophet Isaiah 53:4–6

Surely he has borne our grief and carried our sorrows; yet we esteemed him stricken, smitten by God, and afflicted. But he was wounded for our transgressions, he was bruised for our iniquities; upon him was the chastisement that made us whole, and with his stripes we are healed. All we like sheep have gone astray; we have turned everyone to his own way; and the Lord has laid on him the iniquity of us all.

$\mathcal{M}$an has fallen, and he continues to fall: often he becomes a caricature of himself, no longer the image of God, but a mockery of the Creator. Is not the man who, on the way from Jerusalem to Jericho, fell among robbers who stripped him

 and left him half-dead and bleeding beside the road the image of humanity par excellence? Jesus' fall beneath the cross is not just the fall of the man Jesus, exhausted from his scourging. There is a more profound meaning in this fall, as Paul tells us in the Letter to the Philippians: "Though he was in the form of God, he did not count equality with God a thing to be grasped, but emptied himself, taking the form of a servant, being born in the likeness of men.... He humbled himself and became obedient unto death, even death on a cross" (2:6–8). In Jesus' fall beneath the weight of the cross, the

meaning of his whole life is seen: his voluntary abasement that lifts us up from the depths of our pride. The nature of our pride is also revealed: it is that arrogance which makes us want to be liberated from God and left alone to ourselves, the arrogance that makes us think that we do not need his eternal love, but can  be the masters of our own lives. In this rebellion against truth, in this attempt to be our own god, creator, and judge, we fall headlong and plunge into self-destruction. The humility of Jesus is the surmounting of our pride; by his abasement he lifts us up. Let us allow him to lift us up. Let us strip away our sense of self-sufficiency, our false illusions of independence, and learn from him, the One who humbled himself, to discover our true greatness by bending low before God and before our downtrodden brothers and sisters.

Prayer

Lord Jesus, the weight of the cross made you fall to the ground. The weight of our sin, the weight of our pride, brought you down. But your fall is not a tragedy or mere human weak-ness. You came to us when, in our pride, we were laid low. The arrogance that makes us think that we ourselves can create human beings has turned people into a kind of merchandise to be bought and sold, or stored to provide parts for experimentation. In doing this, we hope to conquer death by our own efforts, yet in reality we are profoundly debasing human dignity. Lord, help us; we have fallen. Help us to abandon our destructive pride and, by learning from your humility, to rise again.

All:

Our Father, who art in heaven,
hallowed be thy name;
thy kingdom come;
thy will be done on earth as it is in heaven.
Give us this day our daily bread;
and forgive us our trespasses
as we forgive those who trespass against us;
and lead us not into temptation,
but deliver us from evil.

Stabat Mater

O quam tristis et afflicta
fuit illa benedica
mater Unigeniti!

Oh, how sad and sore distressed
was that Mother highly blessed
of the sole-begotten One!

✜

Jesus meets his Mother

℣. *Adoramus te, Christe, et benedicimus tibi.*
℞. *Quia per sanctam crucem tuam redemisti mundum.*

℣. *We adore you, O Christ, and we bless you.*
℞. *Because by your holy cross you have redeemed the world.*

From the Gospel according to Luke 2:34–35, 51

Simon blessed them and said to Mary his mother: "Behold, this child is set for the fall and rising of many in Israel, and for a sign that is spoken against (and a sword will pierce through your own soul also), that thoughts of many hearts may be revealed." And his mother kept all these things in her heart.

MEDITATION

On Jesus' Way of the Cross, we also find Mary, his Mother. During his public life she had to step aside to make place for the birth of Jesus'  new family, the family of his disciples. She also had to hear the words: "Who is my mother and who are my brothers?... Whoever does the will of my Father in heaven is my brother, and sister, and mother" (Mt 12:48–50). Now we see her as the Mother of Jesus not only physically, but also in her heart. Even before she conceived him bodily, through her obedience she conceived him in her heart. It was said to Mary: "And behold, you will conceive in your womb and bear a son. He will be great and the Lord God will give to him the throne of his father David" (Lk 1:31ff.). And she would hear from the mouth of the elderly Simeon: "A sword will pierce through your own soul" (Lk 2:35). She would then recall the words of the prophets, words like these: "He was oppressed, and he was afflicted, yet he opened not his mouth; he was like a lamb that is led to slaughter" (Is 54:7). Now it all takes place. In her heart she had kept the words of the angel, spoken to her in the beginning: "Do not be afraid, Mary" (Lk 1:30). The disciples fled, yet she did not flee. She stayed there, with a mother's courage, a mother's fidelity, a mother's goodness, and a faith that did not waver in the hour of dark-

ness: "Blessed is she who believed" (Lk 1:45). "Nevertheless, when the Son of man comes, will he find faith on earth?" (Lk 18:8). Yes, in this moment Jesus knows he will find faith. In this hour, this is his great consolation.

PRAYER

*H*oly Mary, Mother of the Lord, you remained faithful when the disciples fled. Just as you believed the angel's incredible message—that you would become the Mother of the Most High—so too you believed at the hour of his greatest abasement. In this way, at the hour of the cross, at the hour of the world's darkest

night, you became the Mother of all believers, the Mother of the Church. We beg you: teach us to believe, and grant that our faith may bear fruit in courageous service and be the sign of a love ever ready to share suffering and to offer assistance.

All:

Our Father, who art in heaven,
hallowed be thy name;
thy kingdom come;
thy will be done on earth as it is in heaven.
Give us this day our daily bread;
and forgive us our trespasses
as we forgive those who trespass against us;
and lead us not into temptation,
but deliver us from evil.

Stabat Mater

Quae maerebat et dolebat
pia mater, cum videbat
Nati poenas incliti.

Christ above in torment hangs,
she beneath beholds the pangs,
of her dying, glorious Son.

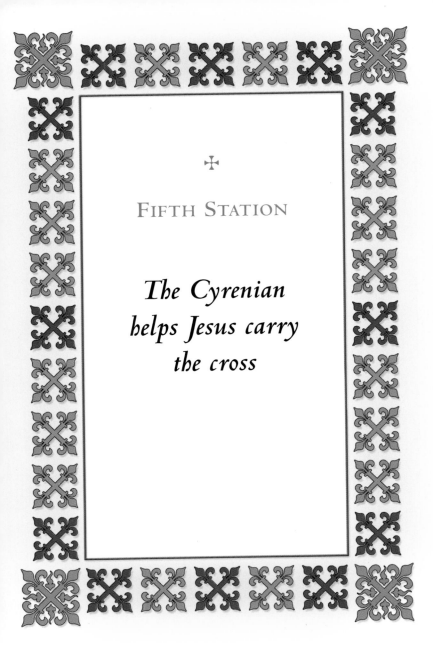

☩

FIFTH STATION

*The Cyrenian
helps Jesus carry
the cross*

℣. *Adoramus te, Christe, et benedicimus tibi.*
℞. *Quia per sanctam crucem tuam redemisti mundum.*

℣. *We adore you, O Christ, and we bless you.*
℞. *Because by your holy cross you have redeemed the world.*

From the Gospel according to Matthew 27:32; 16:24

As they went out, they came upon a man of Cyrene, Simon by name; this man they compelled to carry his cross.

Jesus told his disciples, "If any man would come after me, let him deny himself and take up his cross and follow me."

Simon of Cyrene is on his way home, returning from work, when he comes upon the sad procession of those condemned—for him, perhaps, it was a common sight. The soldiers force this  rugged man from the country to carry the cross on his own shoulders. How annoying he must have thought it to be suddenly caught up in the fate of those condemned men! He does what he must do, but reluctantly. Significantly, the evangelist Mark does not only name him, but also his children, who were evidently known as Christians and as members of that community (cf. Mk 15:21). From this chance encounter faith was born. The Cyrenian, walking beside Jesus and sharing the burden of the cross, came to see that it was a grace to be able to accompany him to his crucifixion and to help him. The mystery of Jesus, silent and suffering, touched his heart. Jesus, whose divine love alone can redeem all humanity, wants us to share his cross so that we can complete what is still lacking in his suffering (cf. Col 1:24). Whenever we show kindness to the suffering, the persecuted, and the defenseless, and share in their sufferings, we help to carry that same cross of Jesus. In this way, we obtain salvation and help contribute to the salvation of the world.

PRAYER

Lord, you opened the eyes and heart of Simon of Cyrene, and you gave him, by his share in your cross, the grace of faith. Help us to aid our neighbors in need, even when this interferes with our own plans and de-  sires. Help us to realize that it is a grace to be able to share the cross of others and, in this way, to know that we are walking with you along the way. Help us to appreciate with joy that when we share in your suffering and the sufferings of this world, we become servants of salvation and are able to help build up your Body, the Church.

All:

Our Father, who art in heaven,
hallowed be thy name;
thy kingdom come;
thy will be done on earth as it is in heaven.
Give us this day our daily bread;
and forgive us our trespasses
as we forgive those who trespass against us;
and lead us not into temptation,
but deliver us from evil.

Stabat Mater

Quis est homo qui non fleret,
matrem Christi si videret
in tanto supplicio?

Is there one who would not weep,
whelmed in miseries so deep,
Christ's dear Mother to behold?

✠

SIXTH STATION

*Veronica wipes
the face of Jesus*

℣. *Adoramus te, Christe, et benedicimus tibi.*
℞. *Quia per sanctam crucem tuam redemisti mundum.*

℣. *We adore you, O Christ, and we bless you.*
℞. *Because by your holy cross you have redeemed the world.*

From the Book of the Prophet Isaiah 53:2–3

He had no form or comeliness that we should look at him, and no beauty that we should desire him. He was despised and rejected by men; a man of sorrows, and acquainted with grief; and as one from whom men hide their faces he was despised, and we esteemed him not.

From the Book of Psalms 27:8–9

You have said, "Seek my face." My heart says to you, "Your face, Lord, do I seek."

Hide not your face from me. Turn not your servant away in anger, you who have been my help. Cast me not off, forsake me not, O God of my salvation.

MEDITATION

"Your face, Lord, do I seek. Hide not your face from me" (Ps 27:8–9). Veronica—Bernice, in Greek tradition—embodies the universal yearning of the devout men and women of the Old  Testament, the yearning of all believers to see the face of God. On Jesus' Way of the Cross, though, she at first did nothing more than perform an act of womanly kindness: she held out a facecloth to Jesus. She did not let herself be deterred by the brutality of the soldiers or the fear that gripped the disciples. She is the image of that good woman, who, amid turmoil and dismay, shows the courage born of goodness and does not allow her heart to be bewildered.

"Blessed are the pure in heart," the Lord had said in his Sermon on the Mount, "for they shall see God" (Mt 5:8). At first, Veronica saw only a buffeted and pain-filled face.  Yet her act of love impressed the true image of Jesus on her heart. On his human face, bloodied and bruised, she saw the face of God and his goodness, which accompanies us even in our deepest sorrows. Only with the heart can we see Jesus. Only love purifies us and gives us the ability to see. Only love enables us to recognize the God who is love itself.

PRAYER

Lord, grant us restless hearts, hearts that seek your face. Keep us from the blindness of heart that sees only the surface of things. Give us the simplicity and purity that allow us to recognize your presence in the world. When we are not able to accomplish great things, grant us the courage that is born of humility and goodness. Impress your face on our hearts. May we encounter you along the way and show your image to the world.

All:

Our Father, who art in heaven,
hallowed be thy name;
thy kingdom come;
thy will be done on earth as it is in heaven.
Give us this day our daily bread;
and forgive us our trespasses
as we forgive those who trespass against us;
and lead us not into temptation,
but deliver us from evil.

Stabat Mater

Pro peccatis suae gentis
vidit Iesum in tormentis
et flagellis subditum.

Bruised, derided, cursed, defiled,
she beheld her tender child,
all with bloody scourges rent.

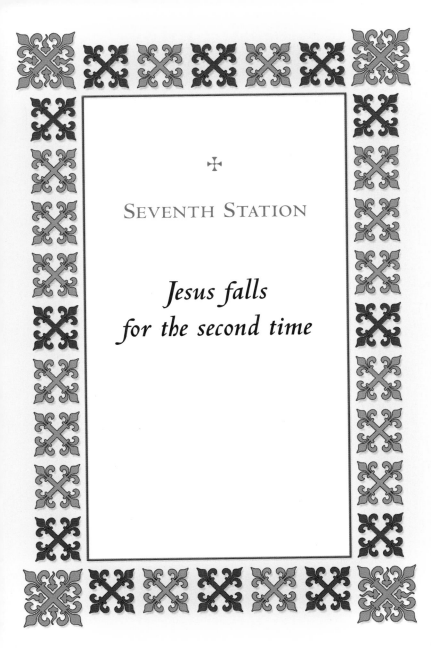

✝

SEVENTH STATION

*Jesus falls
for the second time*

℣. *Adoramus te, Christe, et benedicimus tibi.*
℞. *Quia per sanctam crucem tuam redemisti mundum.*

℣. *We adore you, O Christ, and we bless you.*
℞. *Because by your holy cross you have redeemed the world.*

From the Book of Lamentations 3:1–2, 9, 16

I am the man who has seen affliction under the rod of his wrath; he has driven and brought me into darkness without any light. He has blocked my way with hewn stones; he has made my paths crooked. He has made my teeth grind on gravel, and made me cower in ashes.

MEDITATION

$\mathcal{T}$he tradition that Jesus fell three times beneath the weight of the cross evokes the fall of Adam—the state of fallen humanity—and the mystery of Jesus' own sharing in our fall. Throughout history the fall of man constantly  takes on new forms. In his First Letter, Saint John speaks of a threefold fall: lust of the flesh, lust of the eyes, and the pride of life. He thus interprets the fall of man and humanity against the backdrop of the vices of his own time, with all its excesses and perversions. But we can also think, in more recent times, of how a Christianity grown weary of faith has abandoned the Lord. The great ideologies, and the banal existence of those who, no longer believing in anything, simply drift through life, have built a new and worse paganism, which in its attempt to do away with God once and for all, has ended up doing away with man. And so humanity lies fallen in the dust. The Lord bears this burden and falls, over and over again, in order to meet us. He gazes on us; he touches our hearts; he falls in order to raise us up.

*L*ord Jesus Christ, you have borne all our burdens and you continue to carry us. Our weight has made you fall. Lift us up, for by ourselves we cannot rise from the dust. Free us from the bonds of lust. In place of a heart of stone, give us a heart of flesh, a heart capable of seeing. Lay low the power of ideologies, so that all may see that they are a web of lies. Do not let the wall of materialism become insurmountable. Make  us aware of your presence. Keep us sober and vigilant, capable of resisting the forces of evil. Help us to recognize the spiritual and material needs of others and to give them the help they need. Lift us up, so that we may lift others up. Give us hope at every moment of darkness, so that we may bring your hope to the world.

All:

Our Father, who art in heaven,
hallowed be thy name;
thy kingdom come;
thy will be done on earth as it is in heaven.
Give us this day our daily bread;
and forgive us our trespasses
as we forgive those who trespass against us;
and lead us not into temptation,
but deliver us from evil.

Stabat Mater

Quis non posset contristari,
Christi matrem contemplari,
dolentem cum Filio?

Can the human heart refrain,
from partaking in her pain,
in that Mother's untold pain?

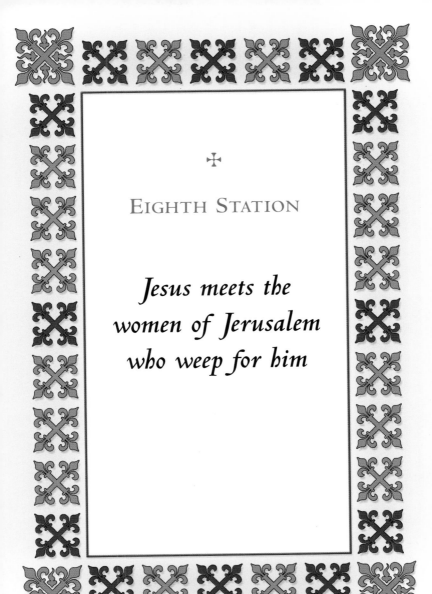

☩

*Jesus meets the
women of Jerusalem
who weep for him*

℣. *Adoramus te, Christe, et benedicimus tibi.*
℟. *Quia per sanctam crucem tuam redemisti mundum.*

℣. *We adore you, O Christ, and we bless you.*
℟. *Because by your holy cross you have redeemed the world.*

From the Gospel according to Luke 23:28–31

Jesus turning to them said, "Daughters of Jerusalem, do not weep for me, but weep for yourselves and for your children. For behold, the days are coming when they will say, 'Blessed are the barren, and the wombs that never bore, and the breasts that never nursed!' Then they will begin to say to the mountains, 'Fall on us'; and to the hills, 'Cover us.' For if they do this when the wood is green, what will happen when it is dry?"

MEDITATION

$\mathcal{H}$earing Jesus reproach the women of Jerusalem who follow him and weep for him ought to make us reflect. How should we understand his words? Are they not directed at  a piety that is purely sentimental, one that fails to lead to conversion and living faith? It is no use to lament the sufferings of this world if our life goes on as usual. And so the Lord warns us of the danger in which we find ourselves. He shows us both the seriousness of sin and the seriousness of judgment. Can it be that, despite all our expressions of consternation in the face of evil and innocent suffering, we are all too prepared to trivialize the mystery of evil? Have we accepted only the gentleness and love of God and Jesus, and quietly set aside the word of judgment? "How can God be so concerned with our weaknesses?" we say. "We are only human!" Yet as we contemplate the sufferings of the Son, we see more clearly the seriousness of sin and how it needs to be fully atoned if it is to be overcome. Before the image of the suffering Lord, evil can no longer be trivialized. To us too, he says: "Do not weep for me, weep for yourselves...if they do this when the wood is green, what will happen when it is dry?"

Prayer

*L*ord, to the weeping women you spoke of repentance and the Day of Judgment, when all of us will stand before your face, before you, the Judge of the world. You call us to leave behind the trivialization of evil, which salves our consciences and allows us to carry on as before. You show us the seriousness of our responsibility, the danger of our being found guilty and without excuse on the Day of Judgment.  Grant that we may not simply walk at your side, with nothing to offer other than compassionate words. Convert us and give us new life. Grant that in the end we will not be dry wood, but living branches in you, the true vine, bearing fruit for eternal life (cf. Jn 15:1–10).

All:

Our Father, who art in heaven,
hallowed be thy name;
thy kingdom come;
thy will be done on earth as it is in heaven.
Give us this day our daily bread;
and forgive us our trespasses
as we forgive those who trespass against us;
and lead us not into temptation,
but deliver us from evil.

Stabat Mater

Tui Nati vulnerati,
tam dignati pro me pati,
poenas mecum divide.

Let me share with you his pain,
who for all my sin was slain,
who for me in torments died.

✠

NINTH STATION

*Jesus falls
for the third time*

℣. *Adoramus te, Christe, et benedicimus tibi.*
℞. *Quia per sanctam crucem tuam redemisti mundum.*

℣. *We adore you, O Christ, and we bless you.*
℞. *Because by your holy cross you have redeemed the world.*

From the Book of Lamentations 3:27–32

It is good for a man that he bear the yoke in his youth. Let him sit alone in silence when he has laid it on him; let him put his mouth in the dust—there may yet be hope; let him give his cheek to the smiter, and be filled with insults. For the Lord will not cast off forever, but, though he cause grief, he will have compassion, according to the abundance of his steadfast love.

MEDITATION

What can the third fall of Jesus under the cross say to us? We have considered the fall of humanity in general, and the falling of many Christians away from Christ and into a godless secularism. Should we not also think of how much Christ suffers in his own Church? How  often is the holy sacrament of his Presence abused, how often must he enter empty and evil hearts! How often do we celebrate only ourselves, without even realizing that he is there! How often is his Word twisted and misused! What little faith is present behind so many theories, so many empty words! How much filth there is in the Church, and even among those who, in the priesthood, ought to belong entirely to him! How much pride, how much self-complacency! What little respect we pay to the sacrament of Reconciliation, where he waits for us, ready to raise us up whenever we fall! All this is present in his passion. His betrayal by his disciples, their unworthy reception of his Body and Blood, is certainly the greatest suffering endured by the Redeemer; it pierces his heart. We can only call to him from the depths of our hearts: *Kyrie eleison*—Lord, save us (cf. Mt 8:25).

Prayer

*L*ord, your Church often seems like a boat about to sink, a boat taking in water on every side. In your field we see more weeds than wheat. The soiled garments and face of your Church throw us into confusion. Yet it is we ourselves who have soiled them! It is we who betray you time and time again, after all our lofty words and grand gestures. Have mercy on your Church; within her, too, Adam contin-ues to fall. When we fall, we drag you down to earth, and Satan laughs, for he hopes that you will not be able to rise from that fall; he hopes that being dragged down in the fall of your Church, you will remain prostrate and overpowered. But you will rise again. You stood up, you arose, and you can also raise us up. Save and sanctify your Church. Save and sanctify us all.

All:

Our Father, who art in heaven,
hallowed be thy name;
thy kingdom come;
thy will be done on earth as it is in heaven.
Give us this day our daily bread;
and forgive us our trespasses
as we forgive those who trespass against us;
and lead us not into temptation,
but deliver us from evil.

Stabat Mater

Eia mater, fons amoris,
me sentire vim doloris
fac, ut tecum lugeam.

O you Mother, fount of love!
Touch my spirit from above,
make my heart with yours accord.

✝

TENTH STATION

Jesus is stripped of his garments

℣. *Adoramus te, Christe, et benedicimus tibi.*
℞. *Quia per sanctam crucem tuam redemisti mundum.*

℣. *We adore you, O Christ, and we bless you.*
℞. *Because by your holy cross you have redeemed the world.*

From the Gospel according to Matthew 27:33–36

And when they came to a place called Golgotha (which means the place of a skull), they offered him wine to drink, mingled with gall, but when he tasted it, he would not drink it. And when they had crucified him, they divided his garments among them by casting lots; then they sat down and kept watch over him there.

Jesus is stripped of his garments. Clothing shows a person's social position; it shows a person's place in society, it makes that person someone. His public stripping means that Jesus is no longer anything at all, he is simply an outcast, despised by all alike. The moment of the  stripping reminds us of the expulsion from Paradise: God's splendor has fallen away from humanity, who now stands naked and exposed, unclad and ashamed. And so Jesus once more takes on the condition of fallen humanity. Stripped of his garments, he reminds us that we have all lost the "first garment," that is, God's splendor. At the foot of the cross, the soldiers draw lots to divide his paltry possessions, his clothes. The evangelists describe the scene with words drawn from Psalm 22:19; by doing so they tell us the same thing that Jesus would tell his disciples on the road to Emmaus: that everything takes place "according to the Scriptures." Nothing is mere coincidence; everything that happens is contained in the Word of God and sustained by his divine plan. The Lord passes through all the stages and steps of humanity's fall from grace, yet each of these steps, for all its bitterness, becomes a step toward our redemption: this is how he carries home the lost sheep. Let us not forget  that John says that lots were drawn for Jesus' tunic, "woven without seam from top to bottom" (Jn 19:23). We may consider this as a reference to the High Priest's robe, which was "woven from a single thread," without stitching (Fl. Josephus, a III, 161). For he, the Crucified One, is the true High Priest.

PRAYER

Lord Jesus, you were stripped of your garments, exposed to shame, cast out of society. You took upon yourself the shame of Adam, and you healed it. You also take upon yourself the sufferings and the needs of the poor, the outcasts of our world. And in this very way  you fulfill the words of the prophets. This is how you bring meaning into apparent meaninglessness. This is how you make us realize that your Father holds you, us, and the whole world in his hands. Give us a profound respect for humanity at every stage of existence and in all the situations in which we encounter people. Clothe us in the light of your grace.

All:

Our Father, who art in heaven,
hallowed be thy name;
thy kingdom come;
thy will be done on earth as it is in heaven.
Give us this day our daily bread;
and forgive us our trespasses
as we forgive those who trespass against us;
and lead us not into temptation,
but deliver us from evil.

Stabat Mater

Fac ut ardeat cor meum
in amando Christum Deum,
ut sibi complaceam.

Make me feel as you have felt,
make my soul to glow and melt,
with the love of Christ our Lord.

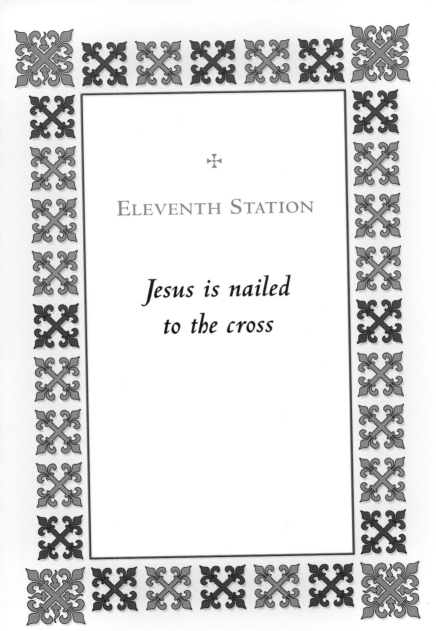

✜

ELEVENTH STATION

*Jesus is nailed
to the cross*

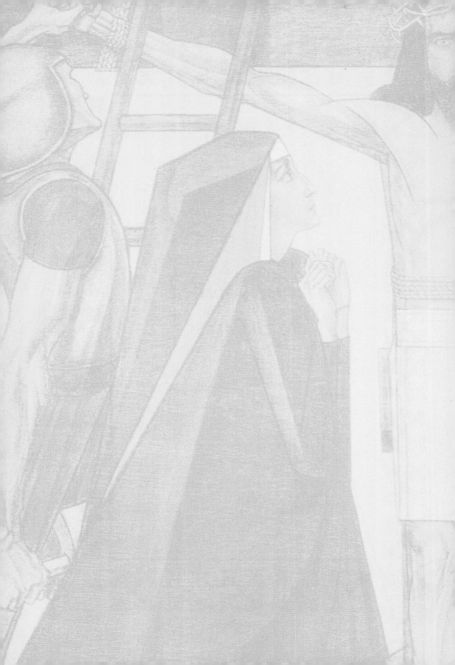

℣. *Adoramus te, Christe, et benedicimus tibi.*

℟. *Quia per sanctam crucem tuam redemisti mundum.*

℣. *We adore you, O Christ, and we bless you.*

℟. *Because by your holy cross you have redeemed the world.*

From the Gospel according to Matthew 27:37–42

And over his head they put the charge against him, which read, "This is Jesus the King of the Jews." Then two robbers were crucified with him, one on the right hand and one on the left. And those who passed by derided him, wagging their heads and saying, "You who would destroy the temple and build it in three days, save yourself! If you are the Son of God, come down from the cross." So also the chief priests with the scribes and elders mocked him, saying, "He saved others; he cannot save himself. He is the King of Israel; let him come down now from the cross and we will believe in him."

MEDITATION

Jesus is nailed to the cross. The shroud of Turin gives us an idea of the unbelievable cruelty of this procedure. Jesus does not drink the numbing gall offered to him; he deliberately takes upon himself all the pain of the crucifixion. His

 whole body is racked; the words of the Psalm have come to pass: "But I am a worm and no man, scorned by men, rejected by the people" (22:7). "As one from whom men hide their faces, he was despised...surely he has borne our grief and carried our sorrows" (Is 53:3ff.). Let us halt before this image of pain, before the suffering Son of God. Let us look upon him at times of presumptuousness and pleasure, in order to learn to respect limits and

to see the superficiality of all merely material goods. Let us look upon him at times of trial and tribulation and realize that it is then that we are closest to God. Let us try to see his face in the people we might look down upon. As we stand before the condemned Lord, who did not  use his power to come down from the cross, but endured its suffering to the end, another thought comes to mind. Ignatius of Antioch, a prisoner in chains for his faith in the Lord, praised the Christians of Smyrna for their invincible faith. He says that they were, so to speak, nailed with flesh and blood to the cross of the Lord Jesus Christ (1:1). Let us nail ourselves to him, resisting the temptation to stand apart or to join others in mocking him.

Prayer

*L*ord Jesus Christ, you let yourself be nailed to the cross, accepting the terrible cruelty of this suffering, the destruction of your body and your dignity. You allowed yourself to be nailed fast; you did not try to escape or to lessen your suffering. May we never flee from what we are called to do. Help us to remain faithful to you. Help us to unmask the false freedom that would distance us from you. Help us to accept your "binding" freedom, and, "bound" fast to you, to discover true freedom.

All:

Our Father, who art in heaven,
hallowed be thy name;
thy kingdom come;
thy will be done on earth as it is in heaven.
Give us this day our daily bread;
and forgive us our trespasses
as we forgive those who trespass against us;
and lead us not into temptation,
but deliver us from evil.

Stabat Mater

Sancta mater, istud agas,
Crucifixi fige plagas
cordi meo valide.

Holy Mother, pierce me through,
in my heart each wound renew,
of my Savior crucified.

✠

TWELFTH STATION

Jesus dies on the cross

℣. Adoramus te, Christe, et benedicimus tibi.

℟. Quia per sanctam crucem tuam redemisti mundum.

℣. We adore you, O Christ, and we bless you.

℟. Because by your holy cross you have redeemed the world.

From the Gospel according to John 19:19–20

Pilate also wrote a title and put it on the cross; it read, "Jesus of Nazareth, the King of the Jews." Many of the Jews read this title, for the place where Jesus was crucified was near the city; and it was written in Hebrew, in Latin, and in Greek.

From the Gospel according to Matthew 27:45–50, 54

Now from the sixth hour there was darkness over all the land until the ninth hour. And about the ninth hour Jesus cried with a loud voice, *"Eli, Eli, lama sabachthani?"* That is, "My God, my God, why have you forsaken me?" And some of the bystanders hearing it said, "This man is calling Elijah." And one of them at once ran and took a sponge, filled it with vinegar, and put it on a reed, and gave it to him to drink. But the others said, "Wait, let us see whether Elijah will come to save him." And Jesus cried again with a loud voice and yielded up his spirit. When the centurion and those who were with him, keeping watch over Jesus, saw the earthquake and what took place, they were filled with awe, and said, "Truly this was the Son of God!"

MEDITATION

*I*n Greek and Latin, the two international languages of the time, and in Hebrew, the language of the Chosen People, a sign stood above the cross of Jesus, indicating who he was: the King of the Jews, the promised Son of David. Pilate, the unjust judge, became a prophet despite himself. The kingship of Jesus was proclaimed before all the world. Jesus himself had not accepted the title "Messiah," because it would have suggested a mistaken, human idea of power and deliverance. Yet now the title can remain publicly displayed above the Crucified Christ. He is indeed the king of the world. Now he is truly "lifted up." In sinking to the depths, he rose to the heights. Now he has radically fulfilled the commandment of love; he  has completed the offering of himself, and in this way he is now the revelation of the true God, the God who is love. Now we know who God is. Now we know what true kingship is. Jesus prays Psalm 22, which begins with the words: "My God, my God, why have you forsaken me?" (v. 2). He takes to himself the whole suffering people of Israel, all of suffering humanity, the drama of God's darkness, and he makes God present in the very place where he seems definitively vanquished and absent. The cross of Jesus is a cosmic event. The world is darkened when the Son of God is given up to death. The earth trembles. And on the cross, the Church of the Gentiles is born. The Roman centurion understands this and acknowledges Jesus as the Son of God. From the cross he triumphs—ever anew.

PRAYER

*L*ord Jesus Christ, at the hour of your death the sun was darkened. Ever anew you are being nailed to the cross. At this present hour of history we are living in God's darkness. Through your great sufferings and the wickedness of  humanity, the face of God, your face, seems obscured, unrecognizable. And yet, on the cross, you have revealed yourself. Precisely by being the one who suffers and loves, you are exalted. From the cross on high you have triumphed. Help us to recognize your face at this hour of darkness and tribulation. Help us to believe in

you and to follow you in our hour of darkness
and need. Show yourself once more to the world
at this hour. Reveal to us your salvation.

All:

Our Father, who art in heaven,
hallowed be thy name;
thy kingdom come;
thy will be done on earth as it is in heaven.
Give us this day our daily bread;
and forgive us our trespasses
as we forgive those who trespass against us;
and lead us not into temptation,
but deliver us from evil.

Stabat Mater

Fac me vere tecum flere,
Crucifixo condolore,
donec ego vixero.

Let me mingle tears with you,
mourning him who mourned for me,
all the days that I may live.

✠

THIRTEENTH STATION

*Jesus is taken down
from the cross
and given
to his Mother*

℣. Adoramus te, Christe, et benedicimus tibi.
℟. Quia per sanctam crucem tuam redemisti mundum.

℣. We adore you, O Christ, and we bless you.
℟. Because by your holy cross you have redeemed the world.

From the Gospel according to Matthew 27:54–55

When the centurion and those who were with him, keeping watch over Jesus, saw the earthquake and what took place, they were filled with awe, and said, "Truly this was the Son of God!" There were also many women there, looking on from afar, who had followed Jesus from Galilee, ministering to him.

*J*esus is dead. From his heart, pierced by the lance of the Roman soldier, flow blood and water: a mysterious image of the stream of the

 sacraments of Baptism and the Eucharist by which the Church is constantly reborn from the opened heart of the Lord. Jesus' legs are not broken like those of the two men crucified

with him. He is thus revealed as the true Paschal Lamb, not one of whose bones must be broken (cf. Ex 12:46). And now, at the end of his sufferings, it is clear that, for all the dismay that filled people's hearts, for all the power of hatred and cowardice, he was never alone. There are faithful ones who remain with him. Under the cross stand Mary, his Mother, the sister of his Mother, Mary, Mary Magdalene, and the disciple whom he loved. A wealthy man, Joseph of Arimathea, appears on the scene: a rich man is able to pass through the eye of a needle, for God has given him the grace. He buries Jesus in his own empty tomb, in a garden. At Jesus' burial, the cemetery becomes a garden, the garden from which Adam was cast out when he abandoned the fullness of life, his Creator. The garden tomb symbolizes that the dominion of death is about to end. A member of the Sanhedrin also comes along, Nicodemus, to whom Jesus had proclaimed the mystery of  rebirth by water and the Spirit. Even in the Sanhedrin, which decreed his death, there is a believer, someone who knows and recognizes Jesus after his death. In this hour of immense grief, of darkness and despair, the light of hope is mysteriously present. The hidden God continues to be the God of life, ever near. Even in the night of death, the Lord continues to be our Lord and Savior. The Church of Jesus Christ, his new family, begins to take shape.

PRAYER

Lord, you descended into the darkness of death. But your body is placed in good hands and wrapped in a white shroud (Mt 27:59). Faith has not completely died; the sun has not completely set. How often does it appear that you  are asleep? How easy it is for us to step back and say to ourselves: "God is dead." In the hour of darkness, help us to know that you are still there. Do not abandon us when we are tempted to lose heart. Help us not to leave you alone. Give us the fidelity to withstand moments of confusion and a love ready to embrace you in your utter helplessness, like your Mother, who once more holds you to her breast. Help us, the poor and rich, simple and learned, to look beyond all our fears and prejudices, and to offer you our abilities, our hearts, and our time, and thus to prepare a garden for the resurrection.

All:

Our Father, who art in heaven,
hallowed be thy name;
thy kingdom come;
thy will be done on earth as it is in heaven.

Give us this day our daily bread;
and forgive us our trespasses
as we forgive those who trespass against us;
and lead us not into temptation,
but deliver us from evil.

Stabat Mater

*Vidit suum dulcem Natum
morientem, desolatum,
cum emisit spiritum.*

For the sins of his own nation
she saw him hang in desolation
till his spirit forth he sent.

✝

FOURTEENTH STATION

*Jesus is laid in
the tomb*

℣. *Adoramus te, Christe, et benedicimus tibi.*
℟. *Quia per sanctam crucem tuam redemisti mundum.*

℣. *We adore you, O Christ, and we bless you.*
℟. *Because by your holy cross you have redeemed the world.*

From the Gospel according to Matthew 27:59–61

Joseph took the body, and wrapped it in a clean linen shroud, and laid it in his own new tomb, which he had hewn in the rock; and he rolled a great stone to the door of the tomb, and departed. Mary Magdalene and the other Mary were there, sitting opposite the sepulcher.

MEDITATION

*J*esus, disgraced and mistreated, is honorably buried in a new tomb. Nicodemus brings a mixture of myrrh and aloes, about a hundred pounds in weight, which gives off a precious scent. In the Son's self-offering, as at his anointing in Bethany, we see an "excess" that evokes  God's generous and superabundant love. God offers himself unstintingly. If God's measure is superabundance, then we for our part should consider nothing too much for God. This is the teaching of Jesus himself in the Sermon on the Mount (Mt 5:20). But we should also remember the words of Saint Paul, who says that God "through us spreads the fragrance of the knowledge of Christ everywhere. We are the aroma of Christ" (2 Cor 2:14ff.). Amid the decay of ideologies, our faith needs once more to be the fragrance that returns us to the path of life. At the very moment of his burial, Jesus' words are fulfilled: "Truly, truly, I say to you, unless a grain of wheat falls to the earth and dies, it remains alone; but if it dies, it bears much fruit" (Jn 12:24). Jesus is the grain of wheat that dies. From that lifeless grain of wheat comes forth the great multiplication of bread that will endure until the end of the world. Jesus is the Bread of Life that can satisfy superabundantly the hunger of all human-ity and provide its deepest nourishment. Through his cross and resurrection, the eternal Word of God became flesh and bread for us. The mystery of the Eucharist already shines forth in the burial of Jesus.

Prayer

Lord Jesus Christ, in your burial you have taken on the death of the grain of wheat. You have become the lifeless grain of wheat that produces abundant fruit for every age and for all eternity. From the tomb shines forth in every generation the promise of the grain of wheat that gives rise to the true manna, the Bread of Life, in which you offer us your very self. The eternal Word, through his incarnation and death, has become a Word that is close to us: you put yourself into our hands and into our hearts, so that your Word can grow within us and bear fruit. Through the death of the grain of wheat you

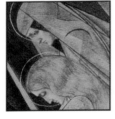 give us yourself, so that we too can dare to lose our life in order to find it; so that we too can trust the promise of the grain of wheat. Help us to grow in love and veneration

for your Eucharistic mystery—to make you, the Bread of Heaven, the source of our life. Help us to become your "fragrance," and to make known in this world the mysterious traces of your life. Like the grain of wheat that rises from the earth, putting forth its stalk and then its ear, you could not remain enclosed in the tomb: the tomb is empty because he—the Father—"did not abandon you to the nether world, nor let your flesh see corruption" (Acts 2:31; Ps 16:10). No, you did not see corruption. You have risen and have made a place for our transfigured flesh in the very heart of God. Help us to rejoice in this hope and to bring it joyfully to the world. Help us to become witnesses of your resurrection.

All:

Our Father, who art in heaven,
hallowed be thy name;
thy kingdom come;
thy will be done on earth as it is in heaven.
Give us this day our daily bread;
and forgive us our trespasses
as we forgive those who trespass against us;
and lead us not into temptation,
but deliver us from evil.

Stabat Mater

Quando corpus morietur,
fac ut animae donetur
paradisi gloria. Amen.

While my body here decays,
may my soul your goodness praise,
safe in paradise with you. Amen.

Blessing

℣. *Dominus vobiscum.*
The Lord be with you.

℞. *Et cum spiritu tuo.*
And also with you.

℣. *Sit nomen Domini benedictum.*
Blessed be the name of the Lord.

℞. *Ex hoc nunc et usque in saeculum.*
Both now and forever.

℣. *Adiutorium nostrum in nomine Domini.*
Our help is in the name of the Lord.

℞. *Qui fecit caelum et terram.*
Who made heaven and earth.

℣. *Benedicat vos omnipotens Deus,*
May Almighty God bless us.
Pater, et Filius, et Spiritus Sanctus.
Father, Son, and Holy Spirit.

℞. Amen.

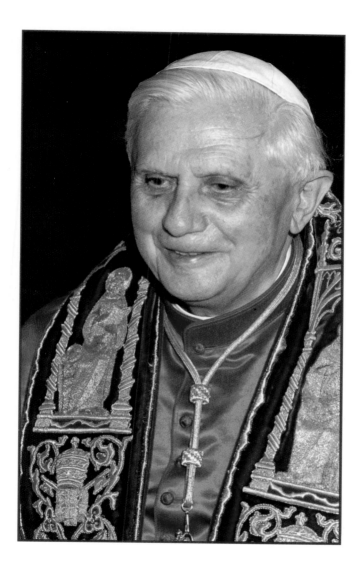

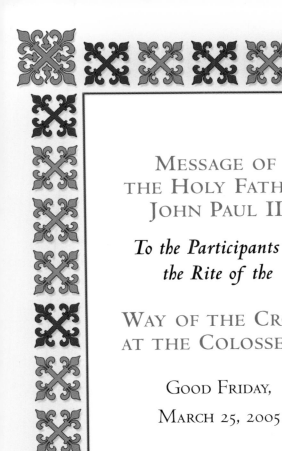

MESSAGE OF THE HOLY FATHER JOHN PAUL II

To the Participants in the Rite of the

WAY OF THE CROSS AT THE COLOSSEUM

GOOD FRIDAY, MARCH 25, 2005

Dear Brothers and Sisters,

I am with you in spirit at the Colosseum, a place that stirs up within me so many memories and emotions, in order to take part in the evocative rite of the Way of the Cross on this Good Friday evening.

I join you in the invocation, so rich in meaning: *"Adoramus te, Christe, et benedicimus tibi, Quia per sanctam crucem tuam redemisti mundum."* Yes, we adore and bless the mystery of the cross of the Son of God, because it was from his death that new hope for humanity was born.

The adoration of the cross directs us to a commitment that we cannot shirk: the mission that Saint Paul expressed in these words: *"[I]n my flesh I complete what is lacking in Christ's afflictions for the sake of his body, that is, the Church"* (Col 1:24). I also offer my sufferings so that God's plan may be completed and his Word spread among the peoples. I, in turn, am close to all who are tried by suffering at this time. I pray for each one of them.

On this memorable day of Christ's crucifixion, I look at the cross with you in adoration, repeating the words of the liturgy: *"O crux, ave spes unica!"* Hail, O cross, our only hope, give us patience and courage and obtain peace for the world!

With these sentiments, I bless you and all those who are taking part in this Way of the Cross via radio or television.

From the Vatican

Joannes Paulus PP. II

BOOKS & MEDIA

The Daughters of St. Paul operate book and media centers at the following addresses. Visit, call or write the one nearest you today, or find us on the World Wide Web, www.pauline.org

CALIFORNIA

3908 Sepulveda Blvd, Culver City,
CA 90230 310-397-8676

5945 Balboa Avenue, San Diego,
CA 92111 858-565-9181

46 Geary Street, San Francisco,
CA 94108 415-781-5180

FLORIDA

145 S.W. 107th Avenue, Miami,
FL 33174 305-559-6715

HAWAII

1143 Bishop Street, Honolulu,
HI 96813 808-521-2731

Neighbor Islands call: 866-521-2731

ILLINOIS

172 North Michigan Avenue,
Chicago, IL 60601 312-346-4228

LOUISIANA

4403 Veterans Memorial Blvd,
Metairie, LA 70006 504-887-7631

MASSACHUSETTS

885 Providence Hwy, Dedham,
MA 02026 781-326-5385

MISSOURI

9804 Watson Road, St. Louis,
MO 63126 314-965-3512

NEW JERSEY

561 U.S. Route 1, Wick Plaza, Edison,
NJ 08817 732-572-1200

NEW YORK

150 East 52nd Street, New York,
NY 10022 212-754-1110

PENNSYLVANIA

9171-A Roosevelt Blvd, Philadelphia,
PA 19114 215-676-9494

SOUTH CAROLINA

243 King Street, Charleston,
SC 29401 843-577-0175

TENNESSEE

4811 Poplar Avenue, Memphis,
TN 38117 901-761-2987

TEXAS

114 Main Plaza, San Antonio,
TX 78205 210-224-8101

VIRGINIA

1025 King Street, Alexandria,
VA 22314 703-549-3806

CANADA

3022 Dufferin Street, Toronto,
ON M6B 3T5 416-781-9131

¡También somos su fuente para libros, videos y música en español!